52 Lessons Every Father Must Teach His Daughter

Corey Pruitt

DEDICATION

This book is dedicated to:

My daughter – Adyson
For being open to learning and growing.
God has big plans for you!

CONTENTS

CHAPTER 1

WHY

Why this book? Why now? These are two questions you may be asking yourself right at this moment. Well, the short answer is, because it is time.

All of us, Fathers, are daily living in the balancing act of life. Balancing mounting work obligations with growing family obligations... balancing hours... balancing finances... balancing relationships... balancing chores... and on, and on.

We live in a busy time of life!

Even though we star in this balancing act, as men we still have a desire to add more to our "show." Our thinking is that more for a little while may equal less time and resource investment in the long run. And, at times, we may be right. Or, our thinking is, this time investment is worth it in the end.

When it comes to the purpose of this book, absolutely, this time and resource investment in your daughter is worth it. The return on your time investment is greater than any stock market return, or business deal. The return on your investment is the integrity and success of your daughter.

What this book is not...
This book is not going to help you by sharing three strategies for managing your work load. Or share seven fool-proof ways to bring happiness to your relationships. This book isn't even going to share with you the elusive

secrets of time management.

What this book is...

This book is your game plan for how you can impact your daughter's life.

Stew on this crazy thought. At work you have project plans, goal sessions and work lists. When you exercise you follow a workout plan or routine. In your finances you have a budget, saving and spending plans. You have retirement plans... business plans... lesson plans... you have meal plans... heck, you probably even have weekend plans!

In all these areas of our lives we have taken some level of calculated effort to reach a pre-defined idea or goal. And, this is a great thing! This is how we, as men and Fathers, manage all that is required of us. But, for some reason we leave the integrity and success of our daughters to chance.

If one does not know to which port one is sailing, no wind is favorable.
Lucius Annaeus Seneca

For some reason, along the path of life, we made the collective decision (often subconsciously) to allow others to have a greater influence on our daughters than we do; others such as teachers, television, magazines, coaches, their friends, their friends' parents, etc.

So, you see, the time is now. The time is now for us to make a calculated effort toward the integrity and success of our daughters. The time is now for us to follow a simple game plan that will yield enormous results.

"The pages in this book have the potential to positively impact the life of your daughter, and your relationship with your daughter."

The 52 lessons that follow are lessons that will impact your daughter on multiple levels. They are lessons that can be learned and reinforced no matter the age of your daughter. And, they are lessons that are best taught by a Father or Father-Figure.

CHAPTER 2

HOW

Don't wait for extraordinary opportunities. Seize common occasions and make them great.
Orison Swett Marden

This book is designed for you to focus on one lesson per week for a year. On the left page you will see the life lesson. On the right page you will see three questions with space to write your thoughts.

- Question #1: How can I best teach my daughter this lesson?
- Question #2: Now that I have taught my daughter this lesson, how can I best reinforce this lesson?
- Question #3: If I were to teach it again, what would I do differently?

These questions are meant to get your "fatherly juices" flowing about the best way to pass the lesson along to your daughter. It is not a lengthy, let's-form-a-committee-and-analyze-this-to-death, process. Rather it is a quick, but calculated, decision process.

Let's unpack these questions a little more, to provide some direction.

Q1: How can I best teach my daughter this lesson?
There are a million ways to teach your daughter. Think about how you might best be able to share this lesson with her. Is it while:

- Playing dolls with her...

- Watching sports...
- Playing sports...
- Putting a Lego structure together...
- Over imaginary tea...
- Out for a special father and daughter date night...
- Sipping on a smoothie or coffee...

Is this lesson better suited for a:
- Face to face conversation (which should be your default)
- Through a phone call
- Through a letter or email

Can you share this lesson through:
- A direct conversation...
- A story about your life that perfectly depicts the lesson...
- A high profile example currently in the media...
- An example of something that happened to her in the past...
- An example of how she could have dealt with something differently...
- A story about one of her friends or a peer she looks up to...

What type of learner is your daughter? Is your daughter more of a
- Visual learner... (show her something)
- Active learner with her body... (have her experience something)
- Auditory learner... (tell her something)

Q2: Now that I have taught my daughter this, how can I best reinforce this lesson?

Your second question is all about reinforcement. Most

lessons will need a little reinforcement. These life lessons are often not a one pop deal. So begin to think about how might you go about reinforcing this lesson in the upcoming weeks?

Also, begin to think about how you might check to see that your daughter caught what you were throwing?

Q3: If I were to teach it again, what would I do differently?

This last question is your time to reflect on what was successful and what bombed. We can spend a lot of time talking about "the big game" and the "dropped passes" on Monday morning, but spend little time reflecting on how the "big game" of being a Father is playing out.

So, think of yourself as the "Monday morning quarterback" of your daughter's success, and reflect on how the lessons are going. What's working? What's not working? What metaphorical balls were dropped by you? What one's were dropped by your daughter? What "passes" of yours just did not hit the mark? And, what passes of yours were right on target.

> *A person who never made a mistake*
> *never tried anything new.*
> *Albert Einstein*

This reflection process is critical to the success of your future lessons, so don't skip this piece of the process.

Jump in...

Well, what are you waiting for? It is time to get started. Don't delay. Don't drag your feet. Don't come up with excuses as to why you can't start now. It all comes down to jumping in!

You can have results or excuses,
you can't have both.
Anonymous

You are not going to get it right every time. You will fumble some weeks, but that is okay. Your daughter is not looking for a polished presentation with corresponding PowerPoint slides. Your daughter is not expecting a sophisticated and refined sales pitch. Your daughter is not even looking for anything remotely close to perfection.

Besides, the worst that can happen is you have an awkward moment with your daughter every once in a while throughout the year...I guarantee your daughter would take awkward moments with you over no moments with you, any day!

There are no secrets to success. It is the result of
preparation, hard work, and learning from failure.
Colin Powell

So, jump in!

Corey Pruitt

CHAPTER 3

THE LESSONS

1
Teach her to laugh

How can I best teach my daughter this lesson?

Now that I have taught my daughter this lesson, how can I best reinforce this lesson?

If I were to teach it again, what would I do differently?

2
Teach her the importance of having her money work for her

How can I best teach my daughter this lesson?

Now that I have taught my daughter this lesson, how can I best reinforce this lesson?

If I were to teach it again, what would I do differently?

3

Teach her to accept compliments with grace and humility

How can I best teach my daughter this lesson?

Now that I have taught my daughter this lesson, how can I best reinforce this lesson?

If I were to teach it again, what would I do differently?

4

Teach her that some males may have different intentions other than what they verbalize

How can I best teach my daughter this lesson?

Now that I have taught my daughter this lesson, how can I best reinforce this lesson?

If I were to teach it again, what would I do differently?

5

Teach her how to pray

How can I best teach my daughter this lesson?

Now that I have taught my daughter this lesson, how can I best reinforce this lesson?

If I were to teach it again, what would I do differently?

6

Teach her the importance of communication

How can I best teach my daughter this lesson?

Now that I have taught my daughter this lesson, how can I best reinforce this lesson?

If I were to teach it again, what would I do differently?

7

Teach her no one ever makes her do, feel, say or think anything…she always has a choice

How can I best teach my daughter this lesson?

Now that I have taught my daughter this lesson, how can I best reinforce this lesson?

If I were to teach it again, what would I do differently?

8

Teach her to respect herself

How can I best teach my daughter this lesson?

Now that I have taught my daughter this lesson, how can I best reinforce this lesson?

If I were to teach it again, what would I do differently?

9

Teach her that it is ok to tell people she loves them

(tell her you love her over and over again…forever)

How can I best teach my daughter this lesson?

Now that I have taught my daughter this lesson, how can I best reinforce this lesson?

If I were to teach it again, what would I do differently?

10

Teach her the importance of family

How can I best teach my daughter this lesson?

Now that I have taught my daughter this lesson, how can I best reinforce this lesson?

If I were to teach it again, what would I do differently?

11

Teach her to have passion about life

How can I best teach my daughter this lesson?

Now that I have taught my daughter this lesson, how can I best reinforce this lesson?

If I were to teach it again, what would I do differently?

12

Teach her that it is ok to have feelings like sad, hurt, angry, happy, love, excitement…and teach her how to positively express those feelings

How can I best teach my daughter this lesson?

Now that I have taught my daughter this lesson, how can I best reinforce this lesson?

If I were to teach it again, what would I do differently?

13

Teach her to pick her friends wisely

How can I best teach my daughter this lesson?

Now that I have taught my daughter this lesson, how can I best reinforce this lesson?

If I were to teach it again, what would I do differently?

14

Teach her that life is not always fair

How can I best teach my daughter this lesson?

Now that I have taught my daughter this lesson, how can I best reinforce this lesson?

If I were to teach it again, what would I do differently?

15

Teach her that expressing herself with well-chosen words always has a better result

How can I best teach my daughter this lesson?

Now that I have taught my daughter this lesson, how can I best reinforce this lesson?

If I were to teach it again, what would I do differently?

16

Teach her about faith

How can I best teach my daughter this lesson?

Now that I have taught my daughter this lesson, how can I best reinforce this lesson?

If I were to teach it again, what would I do differently?

17

Teach her about the benefits of working hard

How can I best teach my daughter this lesson?

Now that I have taught my daughter this lesson, how can I best reinforce this lesson?

If I were to teach it again, what would I do differently?

18

Teach her to be trustworthy and straightforward

How can I best teach my daughter this lesson?

Now that I have taught my daughter this lesson, how can I best reinforce this lesson?

If I were to teach it again, what would I do differently?

19

Teach her to make decisions with the future in mind

How can I best teach my daughter this lesson?

Now that I have taught my daughter this lesson, how can I best reinforce this lesson?

If I were to teach it again, what would I do differently?

20

Teach her to teach herself

How can I best teach my daughter this lesson?

Now that I have taught my daughter this lesson, how can I best reinforce this lesson?

If I were to teach it again, what would I do differently?

21

Teach her the importance of keeping her word

How can I best teach my daughter this lesson?

Now that I have taught my daughter this lesson, how can I best reinforce this lesson?

If I were to teach it again, what would I do differently?

22

Teach her about the power in complimenting others

How can I best teach my daughter this lesson?

Now that I have taught my daughter this lesson, how can I best reinforce this lesson?

If I were to teach it again, what would I do differently?

23

Teach her not to quit out of frustration

How can I best teach my daughter this lesson?

Now that I have taught my daughter this lesson, how can I best reinforce this lesson?

If I were to teach it again, what would I do differently?

24

Teach her to clean up after herself

How can I best teach my daughter this lesson?

Now that I have taught my daughter this lesson, how can I best reinforce this lesson?

If I were to teach it again, what would I do differently?

25

Teach her to be a giver

How can I best teach my daughter this lesson?

Now that I have taught my daughter this lesson, how can I best reinforce this lesson?

If I were to teach it again, what would I do differently?

26

Teach her to respect all people regardless of position, gender or color

How can I best teach my daughter this lesson?

Now that I have taught my daughter this lesson, how can I best reinforce this lesson?

If I were to teach it again, what would I do differently?

27

Teach her to always give 100% in everything she does

How can I best teach my daughter this lesson?

Now that I have taught my daughter this lesson, how can I best reinforce this lesson?

If I were to teach it again, what would I do differently?

28

Teach her to never be afraid to try new things

How can I best teach my daughter this lesson?

Now that I have taught my daughter this lesson, how can I best reinforce this lesson?

If I were to teach it again, what would I do differently?

29

Teach her to celebrate victories and to learn from defeats

How can I best teach my daughter this lesson?

Now that I have taught my daughter this lesson, how can I best reinforce this lesson?

If I were to teach it again, what would I do differently?

30

Teach her the importance of exercise

How can I best teach my daughter this lesson?

Now that I have taught my daughter this lesson, how can I best reinforce this lesson?

If I were to teach it again, what would I do differently?

31

Teach her not to criticize others

How can I best teach my daughter this lesson?

Now that I have taught my daughter this lesson, how can I best reinforce this lesson?

If I were to teach it again, what would I do differently?

32

Teach her that you will always be her biggest fan

How can I best teach my daughter this lesson?

Now that I have taught my daughter this lesson, how can I best reinforce this lesson?

If I were to teach it again, what would I do differently?

33

Teach her to practice patience

How can I best teach my daughter this lesson?

Now that I have taught my daughter this lesson, how can I best reinforce this lesson?

If I were to teach it again, what would I do differently?

34

Teach her how to lose and how to win with humility

How can I best teach my daughter this lesson?

Now that I have taught my daughter this lesson, how can I best reinforce this lesson?

If I were to teach it again, what would I do differently?

35

Teach her that self-worth does not come through the approval of her peers

How can I best teach my daughter this lesson?

Now that I have taught my daughter this lesson, how can I best reinforce this lesson?

If I were to teach it again, what would I do differently?

36

Teach her to forgive, because harboring wrongs is no way to live

How can I best teach my daughter this lesson?

Now that I have taught my daughter this lesson, how can I best reinforce this lesson?

If I were to teach it again, what would I do differently?

37

Teach her to set goals and how to reach them

How can I best teach my daughter this lesson?

Now that I have taught my daughter this lesson, how can I best reinforce this lesson?

If I were to teach it again, what would I do differently?

38

Teach her about moderation

How can I best teach my daughter this lesson?

Now that I have taught my daughter this lesson, how can I best reinforce this lesson?

If I were to teach it again, what would I do differently?

39

Teach her to be accountable for her decisions and actions

How can I best teach my daughter this lesson?

Now that I have taught my daughter this lesson, how can I best reinforce this lesson?

If I were to teach it again, what would I do differently?

40

Teach her how to work for what she really wants

How can I best teach my daughter this lesson?

Now that I have taught my daughter this lesson, how can I best reinforce this lesson?

If I were to teach it again, what would I do differently?

41

Teach her to be humble

How can I best teach my daughter this lesson?

Now that I have taught my daughter this lesson, how can I best reinforce this lesson?

If I were to teach it again, what would I do differently?

42

Teach her to have big dreams

How can I best teach my daughter this lesson?

Now that I have taught my daughter this lesson, how can I best reinforce this lesson?

If I were to teach it again, what would I do differently?

43

Teach her that God answers prayer

How can I best teach my daughter this lesson?

Now that I have taught my daughter this lesson, how can I best reinforce this lesson?

If I were to teach it again, what would I do differently?

44

Teach her to keep commitments

How can I best teach my daughter this lesson?

Now that I have taught my daughter this lesson, how can I best reinforce this lesson?

If I were to teach it again, what would I do differently?

45

Teach her that her thoughts will determine her actions and attitudes

How can I best teach my daughter this lesson?

Now that I have taught my daughter this lesson, how can I best reinforce this lesson?

If I were to teach it again, what would I do differently?

46

Teach her that she is capable to accomplish anything

How can I best teach my daughter this lesson?

Now that I have taught my daughter this lesson, how can I best reinforce this lesson?

If I were to teach it again, what would I do differently?

47

Teach her about Jesus

How can I best teach my daughter this lesson?

Now that I have taught my daughter this lesson, how can I best reinforce this lesson?

If I were to teach it again, what would I do differently?

48

Teach her the words "impossible" and "never" are not a part of her vocabulary

How can I best teach my daughter this lesson?

Now that I have taught my daughter this lesson, how can I best reinforce this lesson?

If I were to teach it again, what would I do differently?

49

Teach her that preparation + determination = success

How can I best teach my daughter this lesson?

Now that I have taught my daughter this lesson, how can I best reinforce this lesson?

If I were to teach it again, what would I do differently?

50

Teach her there is no value in jealousy, but great value in thankfulness

How can I best teach my daughter this lesson?

Now that I have taught my daughter this lesson, how can I best reinforce this lesson?

If I were to teach it again, what would I do differently?

51

Teach her that what she feeds her thoughts is what she will get in return

How can I best teach my daughter this lesson?

Now that I have taught my daughter this lesson, how can I best reinforce this lesson?

If I were to teach it again, what would I do differently?

52

Teach her that, even though she is good at something, there is always room to improve

How can I best teach my daughter this lesson?

Now that I have taught my daughter this lesson, how can I best reinforce this lesson?

If I were to teach it again, what would I do differently?

CHAPTER 4

WHAT NOW?

Well, what now? Wash, rinse, repeat! Start back at lesson one and do it all over again. Read what you wrote for your questions #2 and #3. Make changes as necessary... and... enjoy the journey!

ABOUT THE AUTHOR

Corey is most proud of being a father of 4 kids (three sons and a daughter). He is a self-proclaimed "Father in training" as he learns on the job.

Corey is a thought leader and innovator specializing in professional and personal development, strategic communication, motivation and performance improvement.

He is a highly motivated, nationally known speaker and trainer. He has a keen ability to inspire new learning, facilitate new actions and impact change. His work transforms both people and businesses.

Corey draws from his experience as a counselor, Business Owner, Motivation and Performance Trainer, Communication and Psychology Professor, and various leadership positions in higher education.